I Am Not Your Enemy

The Body of Christ Divided

L. Y. Njie

Copyright © 2014 L. Y. Njie

All rights reserved.

ISBN-13: 978-0615977027

DEDICATION

This book is dedicated to my mother who always believed in me and my father who always stressed the importance of prayer.

CONTENTS

Preface

1 The Purpose   1-3

2 Mingling With The World   4-7

3 Blinded Eyes   8-10

4 The Illusion   11-14

5 The Trouble   15-17

6 Reclaiming The Position   18-22

Preface

" A house divided against itself cannot stand." This is a famous line from a speech that was delivered by Abraham Lincoln as he ran against Stephen A. Douglas for the U.S. Senate in 1858. Mr. Lincoln was chosen by Republican delegates because it was believed that he was the most likely candidate to defeat the Democrats in the senatorial race. However, things did not turn out the way the Republicans anticipated.

It was believed by some that the speech Abraham Lincoln delivered, which included the above referenced clause, cost the Republicans the election. The general consensus was that the language was harsh and inappropriate for the occasion. The Republican senatorial candidate was viewed as being morally courageous but politically incorrect.

The words in the speech were very carefully chosen by Abraham Lincoln. He obtained the idea for the aforementioned clause from the words of Jesus written in the Bible. Mr. Lincoln wanted to share a message with the people that would be very compelling from an equally compelling personage.

His purpose was to alert the people to the peril of the times during slavery. He wanted to cast light upon the notion that the States would not be able to successfully continue its existence having divided views with regard to slavery. His warning was fueled with the intent of bringing the attention of mankind to the imminent implosion that was inevitable within in the American states.

The house of America was divided by the ideology of the North and that of the South and it was about to fall like a house of cards. The war that was waged within its walls should not have happened. However, ignorance and obstinate personalities were given free course to fester and culminate in a Civil War because the two sides were not willing to come to a compromise which would have benefitted those living in the States. Instead each side was adamant about retaining its measure of the power.

1

The Purpose

"And he saith unto them, Go ye into all the world, and preach the gospel to every creature." – Mark 16:15

The original purpose of the church was evangelical in nature. The plan put in place by Jesus before He left the earth was to have the Gospel, also known as the Good News of salvation, spread throughout the world. It was not His desire for anyone to be lost in a life of sin because they were not afforded the opportunity of a relationship with Him.

The disciples of Jesus Christ were mandated to spread the Word of God in their hometown as well as abroad. The intention was to be able to advance the Kingdom of God on earth and the only way to do that was to be busy at all times sharing the Gospel with everyone who was willing to Hear.

In its most elementary stage of existence, the church was a place where the followers of Jesus Christ could assemble together and hear the Word of God preached while giving glory to the God they loved. It was a place where all things were common—meaning everyone shared their belongings with the church. No one person kept his property for himself but the rights to the property were given over by the owner so that anyone in the congregation who was lacking was able to receive sustenance.

It was in the church that miracles were experienced. These supernatural happenings were prevalent in the church because of the prayer that went on continually. Love was also prevalent in the midst of those who gathered to enjoy the presence of God, which helped to provide an atmosphere for the manifestation of the miracles.

Another purpose of the church was to foster an atmosphere where those who were outcast because of their faith in Jesus Christ could gather together, love one another, take care of others, and exemplify their faith to others. All that were afflicted were brought to the church for the purpose of being freed from the chains of their infirmities. No one was ostracized because of an ailment they suffered from—whether it was mental or physical the church was the hospital where all manner of healings would take place. When the Saints prayed in the old church, the dead were raised and the prison doors were opened for the brethren which were wrongly accused.

The Saints in the early church waited with great expectation for the second coming of Jesus Christ to rapture them from the earth. They lived everyday as if it were their last with the anticipation of His return. This type of lifestyle caused them to operate with one another in love because they did not want to miss the blessed event when they would be able to go back with Jesus and be with Him in Glory. They were living to live again in eternity with Jesus.

2

Mingling With The World

"No man can serve two masters: for either he will hate the one, and love the other; or else he will hold to the one and despise the other. Ye cannot serve God and mammon." – Matthew 6:24

The modern church has found itself in a perplexing dilemma. Many in the Body of Christ continue to gather together in the name of Jesus Christ but the dedication to the cause has been lost. Sunday service still goes on as usual but the purpose behind the meeting of the Saints has definitely changed. No longer is the main purpose of the church as a whole, the advancing of the Kingdom of God.

A large number of churches are very concerned about issues that have nothing to do with the Gospel of Jesus Christ. Money and designer outfits have become more important than leading souls to the Kingdom of God. More than a few church leaders are primarily concerned about collecting a large offering. The subject of the spiritual health of their congregation is not a top priority. They will allow everything that is contrary to the Word of God to take place in their church with their congregants and not teach against it. The Bible is not taught or preached in a thorough manner because they do not want to upset their biggest tippers. I phrase it this way because this is what the offering has become. It has become a tipping system for the preacher in most assemblies. If a preacher can make you jump out of your seat and stand on your feet for the duration of the message, he is usually generously rewarded monetarily. It does not matter whether he is speaking the truth or not. As long as the man of God can make everyone feel good he is worthy of a large offering and many accolades.

The prophet that constantly gives words of prosperity will always have a large following. People have fallen in love with the thought of becoming rich and famous on the wings of the prophetic words which proceed out of the mouth of those whom they view to be God's anointed. Everyone wants a miracle to fall from the sky. No one wants to seek the face of God anymore.

I am not insinuating that the laborer is not worthy of his wages (I Timothy 5:18) but the collection plate has become more than a means by which the man of God is taken care of for doing his job and working as a constant intercessor for the people. It is the responsibility of the leaders in the church to be the ones on the front line losing sleep at night as he or she is going to God on the behalf of their congregants and others. They should preach and teach the word in truth regardless of what it means for the amount of money they will receive in the offering.

I also believe many of the pastors and preachers are hesitant to speak the truth because they are afraid the praise will stop. Unfortunately, a significant number of leaders in the church are self ordained leaders that failed in the secular realm so they came to God in search of an identity. If they preach the truth, the calls may stop and they will become an invisible personality among the Saints just as they were in the world. They fall hard because their self-esteem issues should have been dealt with before becoming a leader in the Lord's church.

There are also the congregants who have made the church into their runway and social club. The only reason they attend service is to showcase their latest outfit and talk about the person who does not have on something new. The brother or sister that is hurting is overlooked because the motive of the one sitting next to them is not in line with the Bible's instruction to love one another and to treat others as you would want to be treated.

Searching for your next victim to sleep with should not be a motive for attending church, but it has become one of the reasons people find themselves in service on Sunday. Even though this should not be the case, it is taking place openly because many leaders are not teaching the Bible.

We have fallen into the trap of believing that many of the teachings of the Bible are obsolete and we find ourselves inventing new philosophical views to interpret the Word of God. As a result, people feel comfortable doing whatever makes them happy with no regard for the Word of God or the plan of salvation.

The church has now become a pious copy of the world. Instead of the world copying us, we are mimicking all of their actions. We lie, cheat, steal, fornicate, commit adultery, commit murder-spiritual and physical and we still stick our chests out and call ourselves Christians. However, we do not display any of the birthmarks of one that has been born again of the water and the spirit.

3

Blinded Eyes

"Having eyes, see you not? And having ears, hear ye not? and do ye not remember?"
—Mark 8:18

In spite of everything that is happening in the world, the church still has not realized the error of its ways. Service after service we gather together with the form of godliness but we are denying the power that comes along with wearing the name of Jesus Christ as Christians. We deny the power by not operating in love thus forfeiting the miracles that the followers of Christ should be experiencing on a regular basis.

The Bible admonishes that prayer go forth for all men in order to allow us the luxury of a peaceful existence.

(I Timothy 2:1-3) Chaos and tragedies have become commonplace in our society and we have closed our eyes and turned up our noses. We often comment that something unfortunate happened to someone because they were not a believer or because they did something to deserve it. Why have we not realized that tragedies happen to the just and the unjust? We have not been diligent in our duties of prayer.

Burying our heads in the sand will not cause the circumstances in our lives and the lives of our loved ones to change. All of the warnings are in the Bible and we still have not been able to recognize what is taking place or the solution for the problem.

In times of peril, the world will often turn to the church for answers to problematic situations. However, most of the times we have nothing concrete to offer as we are mocked by the questions, because we are not praying or studying the Word of God. The only available response we are able to provide is they should have faith and that one cannot always understand why God allows certain things to happen. An individual that is hurting and looking for answers needs to hear more than a rehearsed line that we do not live by in our own times of crisis. They need to hear the words of God being delivered by someone who has spent time with Him.

It is an honor and a privilege to be able to spend time in the presence of the King of Kings. It is in His presence that we receive power to face the day and to be a help to others. The patience we need to deal with the spouse, the boss and the kids is all found in His presence. However, we will never realize the effects of a relationship with God if we continue to pretend that we do not need to acknowledge Him in all of our ways so that He can direct our paths. We will never be able to experience the upside of life unless we take our blinders off and admit the need we have to seek God for everything.

God is the key to all of our problems. All of the answers are with Him. He created all of us, so He understands who we are and how we operate. If we seek Him, He will be more than willing to share the secrets of life with us.

4

The Illusion

"For we wrestle not against flesh and blood, but against principalities, against powers, against the rulers of the darkness of this world, against spiritual wickedness in high places." –Ephesians 6:12

The lack of prayer in the lives of Christians has caused a civil war to break out within the church. We fight against one another even though we should love one another. Jealousy and envy are running rampant in the congregation of the Saints as well. Hatred has reared its ugly head along with cynicism and distrust.

We are so busy being at odds with one another we are not

focusing on the matters at hand. The person sitting next to you is not your enemy. The spirit that is operating in the person is your enemy. We spend a lot of time being distracted by the petty disagreements because we are not bringing these things to God in prayer on a regular basis. Situations that are dealt with in prayer on a continual basis do not have the chance to take root in your life.

The spirits that are causing the disruptions in your life are able to operate and be so successful because we are not spending time with God in prayer. Instead of praying, we get on the telephone and call our friend so that we can discuss how we were done wrong. We are hurt because we misunderstood the actions of someone else so we are going to tarnish their character in a conversation with a friend. Even the secular world knows that two wrongs don't make a right.

A lot of misunderstandings come from the fact that we have a hard time coming to the realization that the world does not revolve around us. We forget that the person who hurt us has an existence outside of the time they spend around us. Perhaps, there are circumstances that have presented themselves in their lives that they cannot handle. It could be that they lost their job or their spouse walked out on them. The reason they did not speak after service on Friday is because they had to use all the strength they had left to keep from crying. However, it is difficult for us to understand this because there are so many issues and spirits to be dealt with that it is hard to think straight. Everyone is not plotting against one another to embarrass or undermine the next person's grandeur.

The world is in need of prayers to go up in order to war against everything that is occurring today but we are too busy warring against one another. The battle is being waged in the spiritual. We will never be able to be effective if we do not fight the battle on the proper front. We cannot fight a spiritual battle in the natural realm. We need to see beyond the person and ask God to give us discernment into the situation or spirit that is causing the actions we are witnessing.

When we learn to love one another anything is possible. In a loveless state we do not care to know the reason for a person's actions. We are ready and willing to confront anyone that offends us.

However, when I love my neighbor I care about their well being more than my pride. When love is present I will pray for them before I decide to not speak to them for a misunderstanding that could be solved by communication. Prayer is the key to love which is the key to winning the battle against the unseen forces.

I Corinthians 13 states that without love all of the gifts in operation are null and void. Love will allow us to operate in the gifts of the spirit and realize the manifestation of God's overcoming power in our life. It will also cause us to see the people and their actions for what they are. We will be able to separate the person from the spirit when we have a life of prayer.

When we adopt prayer as a way of life, our actions will become more deliberate. We will be able to walk in faith and not in fear. Our lives will be transformed because we will not be able to be controlled like a puppet by the circumstances and situations we encounter. Spending time with God in prayer will cause us to enjoy the privilege of being able to speak to the spirits and cause them to cease their actions which will allow us to operate freely in the manner God intended. There are many things that are set up for the Christian to enjoy but we are not able to obtain these things because our progress is in impeded by the war being waged against us in the spiritual realm.

5

The Trouble

"And Jesus knew their thoughts, and said unto them, Every kingdom divided against itself is brought to desolation; and every city or house divided against itself shall not stand:" -Matthew 12:25

The respect the church once enjoyed has been lost in a barrage of scandals and folly. No one can take us seriously anymore. The world would rather consult the psychic for answers instead of the religious leaders. We have been relegated to a group of people that shout and scream for no reason because after all of the bodily exercise we still do not have the answers to the pertinent questions of life.

Where are the Daniels and Josephs among the redeemed?

These are those that interpret dreams and are able to explain the mysteries of God. These have dedicated themselves to a life of prayer, which is not a chore, but a privilege in which they enjoy partaking because of their love for God.

Psychics have become one of the major sources people seek out when they have dilemmas they cannot solve. The world has bypassed God and gone straight to the psychic because the church is not operating in the power it was meant to have. Life changing moments are not taking place as much as they should. One may witness a miracle on a special occasion but it is not common place. People are seeking for answers and the church should be leading the world to prayer. However, we cannot lead anyone to prayer because we do not pray ourselves.

We should be operating as one cohesive unit. God did not intend for there to be division within the Body of Christ. (1 Corinthians 1:10) As we fight with one another we allow the enemy of our soul to come in with his plan of attack and destroy us before we reach our destiny.

We are so busy at each other's throats, we do not realize that a major attack plan has been plotted against our leaders. If the devil can destroy the leaders he can destroy us because we will be like sheep without a covering. Sheep are not very smart animals and they need a shepherd to lead them in the right direction. Jesus being the Great Shepherd has put in place pastors in the position of under shepherds in order to steer us in the way of truth.

The church is no longer a threat to the powers of darkness because we do not pray, we don't love and we do not read the word of God. These are the things that build us up and allow us to fight against the powers of evil. Due to a lack of proper spiritual dietary habits, malnutrition has set in and we are wasting away. Every church is not in this predicament but most of the churches have already fallen or are headed for this pattern.

Although God gave us everything we needed to maintain our existence, we are beginning to come apart at the seams. Abraham Lincoln, in the speech he made when he ran for the United States Senate in 1858, realized that a house against itself would not stand. Although there were those that did not agree with his choice to deliver this speech, he chose to do it because he wanted the people to understand the peril of the times they were living in. He decided to say the unpopular thing in order to enlighten the public. This is where we have lost it. Instead of preaching about the perils of the times we are in, the preacher is preaching about God blessing everyone with a new house or car while we cannot learn to get along with each other. We cannot get past the fact that someone that is not part of our clique sat in a seat on the row we sit on every Sunday. The church is on its way to imploding and we continue to be divided over petty differences.

The Bible speaks about not being able to put new wine into old bottles because the bottles would not be able to handle it and they would break. Only new bottles would be able to house the new wine. In the exact same manner, God is not able to do anything new for us if we do not move past our old mind set. We would never be able to appreciate the handiwork of God in the state that we are in.

6

Reclaiming the Position

"Be not overcome of evil, but overcome evil with good."- Romans 12:21

Although the church is in a less than glorified position right now, all is not lost. God is merciful and forgiving and intends for the Gospel to be shared throughout the world so that everyone has the chance to know Him in a personal relationship. His intention does not change because we refuse to cooperate.

Jesus is waiting for us to turn to Him to change things. Some of us may know or maybe we have forgotten about the weapons that God has given to us to be able to survive on this earth. Three of the most powerful weapons are prayer, praise, and the Word. Prayer is our primary mode of communicating with God. God knows everything before we come to Him but He enjoys spending time with His children. When we offer up praise to God we give God a vehicle by which he is able to intervene in our situations. God inhabits the praise of Israel or those that are believers. (Psalm 22:3)The Word, as a weapon, allows us to know what we are fighting and how to fight. God gives us instruction by way of His Word. There is no situation occurring in our lives or in the modern world that the Bible does not cover. The situations are the same but the characters are different.

The church has witnessed the power of God when engaging in corporate prayer. Individual prayer is great but God does something magnificent when His people get together for the purpose of seeking Him and they are all on one accord. The church prayed without ceasing for Peter's release from prison and God sent an angel to release Him before He was supposed to stand trial before Herod. Herod was evil and intended to persecute the followers of Christ but prayer delivered Peter from a grim fate. (Acts 12:1-17) When Paul and Silas were in prison for being led by the Spirit and ruining the livelihood of a few ungodly men, at midnight they prayed and sang praises to God. As they did this, an earthquake shook the foundations of the prison and all the prisoners were loosed—not only Paul and Silas. (Acts 16:16-40)

Hope is not lost. If we lift up our voices in prayer, praise and adoration for God, He is willing to work miracles and pull us out of the ominous quick sand we have allowed ourselves to be caught in. The key to the rescue is consistency. We have to seek God on a consistent basis in order to stop the sinking effect. As we pray, He pulls us up but when we neglect to keep our half of the deal we are in danger of slipping into an abyss of troubles that will wash over our heads like a tidal wave. We need to seek God without ceasing.

It is also imperative that we stick to the Bible and its doctrine as it has been presented to us. Some congregations have developed the practice of changing the basis of their teaching along with the newest fad going around in Christendom. We get distracted by all of the different doctrines being created and we lose sight of our focal point which is the advancement of the Kingdom. The skin color of God is not relevant nor should His gender be a topic for debate. The important thing is the world is dying in sin and the church should be instrumental in spreading the good news about the plan of salvation.

An inordinate amount of time is spent trying to prove each other wrong about petty points in dogma. We are fighting amongst ourselves while our common enemy is operating undetected. The devil hates anyone who has access to God so while we fight against our brother and allow ourselves to be used by the enemy, his purpose is being advanced while God's is being impeded.

As believers, we should watch as well as pray so that we will be alert and sensitive to the move of God. Careful thought should be exercised in every move that is made regarding the church. Consult God for direction in appointing candidates for offices in the church. We work against ourselves when we allow someone to hold an office for which they are not suitable. This causes a vacancy in the position although it has been filled because the person will not be able to operate properly in an office for which they are not anointed to serve.

All night prayer should be taking place in the churches. It is during the hours between midnight and 6a.m. that we should be engaging God in conversation. This is the time when most of the work is done in the spiritual realm. During these hours your destiny for the next day is worked out.

We also need to be business minded, understanding that people are judging us by how we conduct ourselves with mankind. Understand that we are being watched and scrutinized very closely. We must watch our moves and walk the chalk line in order to gain the respect of those in the secular society. For instance, if we have a business we need to deliver on the product or service and provide quality. We have a bad reputation of being negligent in matters of business.

Jealousy is another vice that needs to be addressed. In the church, we become covetous of the position of others because we are not content with ourselves. It needs to be understood that the most important thing is a relationship with God. The Bible admonishes that we should first seek the Kingdom of God and His righteousness and all other ancillary things like our desires will be added to us. (Matthew 6:33) When we follow God's prescribed way we are legally able to obtain everything He has for us because we are submitted to His authority. When we are not submitted to God, we leave ourselves open to the attack of the enemy – whether spiritual or physical.

Also, invading the church like the stench of a dead rat, is the notion of not forgiving. When we are offended by our brothers or sisters in Christ we are supposed to deal with the problem and forgive them. (Matthew 18:21-22) I am not insinuating that this is easy but it is important for us to have mercy on others if we want to experience mercy from others and God. I know there are those that feel they are perfect and do not need mercy from anyone. However, remember that all of mankind is born in sin and shapen in iniquity (Psalm 51:5) and with sin comes guaranteed imperfections.

It is possible for us to regain the position of respect the church once held, however it will take hard work, dedication and consistent prayer. I cannot stress the importance of prayer enough. The lack of prayer is what allowed us to fall to the position we are in now. If we pray and seek the Almighty , Omniscient God He is willing and able to lift us up back into the place of prominence and respect we once held as Christians in the Lord's Church.

ABOUT THE AUTHOR

La Shan Y. Njie was born in Manhattan and raised in the Bronx, NY. She is an ordained minister and is currently a member of the Queens location of the Rehoboth Apostolic Assemblies, Inc.

www.ingramcontent.com/pod-product-compliance
Lightning Source LLC
Chambersburg PA
CBHW051720040426
42446CB00008B/983